Washington, DC

BY MARI KESSELRING

The Child's World

Published by The Child's World®
1980 Lookout Drive • Mankato, MN 56003-1705
800-599-READ • www.childsworld.com

ACKNOWLEDGMENTS
The Child's World®: Mary Berendes, Publishing Director
The Design Lab: Design and production
Red Line Editorial: Editorial direction

PHOTO CREDITS: iStockphoto, cover, 1, 3; Matt Kania/Map Hero, Inc., 4, 5;
David Kay/Shutterstock Images, 7; Cheng Chang/iStockphoto, 9; Bigstock,
10; Photolibrary, 11; Jon Elswick/AP Images, 13; San Rostro/Photolibrary, 15;
Albert de Bruijn/iStockphoto Images, 17; Jae C. Hong/AP Images, 19; Asier
Villafranca/Shutterstock Images, 21; One Mile Up, 22; Quarter-dollar coin
image from the United States Mint, 22

LIBRARY OF CONGRESS CATALOGING-IN-PUBLICATION DATA
Kesselring, Mari.
  Washington, DC / by Mari Kesselring.
    p. cm.
  Includes bibliographical references and index.
  ISBN 978-1-60253-493-3 (library bound : alk. paper)
  1. Washington (D.C.)—Juvenile literature. I. Title.

F194.3.K47 2010
975.3—dc22

2010017712

Printed in the United States of America in Mankato, Minnesota.
July 2010
F11538

On the cover:
The Washington
Monument
is 555 feet
(169 m) tall.

CONTENTS

Geography

Let's explore Washington, DC! It is in the east-central United States. Washington, DC is between Maryland and Virginia.

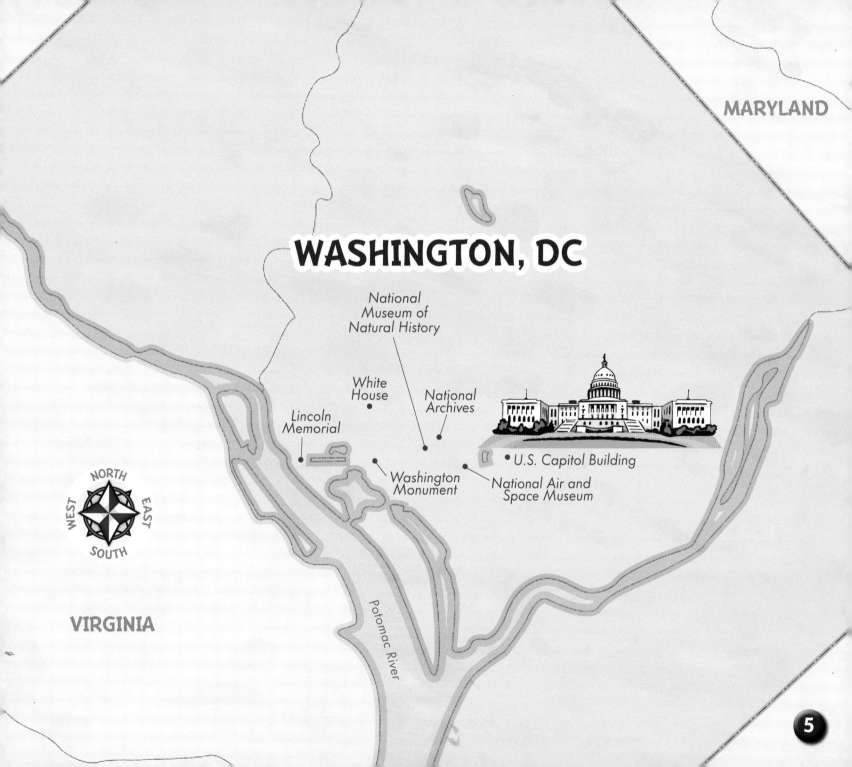

MARYLAND

WASHINGTON, DC

National
Museum of
Natural History

White
House

National
Archives

Lincoln
Memorial

NORTH
WEST
EAST
SOUTH

Washington
Monument

• U.S. Capitol Building

National Air and
Space Museum

VIRGINIA

Potomac River

Cities

DC stands for **District** of Columbia. Washington is the only city on this special piece of land. Washington, DC is the capital of the United States. It is not one of the 50 states.

The U.S. Capitol Building (far left) and the Lincoln **Memorial** (left) can be seen from the Potomac River. ▶

Land

Washington, DC covers only 100 square miles (260 square km). The land in Washington, DC is mostly flat. The Potomac River is its southwest border.

Cherry trees **bloom** on the banks of the Potomac River. ▶

Plants and Animals

The official bird of Washington, DC is the wood thrush. It is a songbird. The official tree is the scarlet oak. Washington, DC's flower is the American beauty rose.

American beauty roses open in late summer and fall. ▶

People and Work

More than 500,000 people live in Washington, DC. Many people work for the government. Many people also work in **tourism**.

Guides help visitors at the National Archives Building. This building houses the Declaration of Independence ▶ and other important documents.

History

President George Washington chose this area for the country's capital in 1790. Before this, the U.S. government's offices were in Philadelphia, Pennsylvania.

George Washington was president of the ▶
United States from 1789 to 1797.

George Washington did not live in the city of Washington while he was president. After his presidency, in 1800, the city became the country's capital.

Ways of Life

Washington, DC is home to the main government offices of the United States. Many people study and talk about **politics**. People enjoy learning about the area's history.

The presidents of the United States and their families ▶ have lived in the White House since the early 1800s.

Famous People

Former U.S. Vice President Al Gore was born in Washington, DC. Actress Katherine Heigl was also born here. **Jazz** musician Duke Ellington was born here, too. Important world leaders often visit Washington, DC to talk to U.S. government leaders.

Al Gore speaks to an audience about the environment. ▶

Famous Places

Washington, DC has many places to see. People can take **tours** of the White House and the U.S. Capitol Building. Washington, DC has memorials. These are places that honor people or events. The Lincoln Memorial and the Vietnam Veterans Memorial Wall are **popular** places to visit.

The Lincoln Memorial honors Abraham Lincoln, ▶ the sixteenth president of the United States.

Symbols

Seal

The woman on Washington, DC's seal stands for **justice**. She stands next to a **statue** of George Washington. Go to childsworld.com/links for a link to Washington, DC's Web site, where you can get a firsthand look at the seal.

Flag

The flag is based on President George Washington's personal **coat of arms**.

Quarter

Washington, DC's quarter shows an image of jazz musician Duke Ellington. It also displays Washington, DC's **motto**, "Justice For All." The quarter came out in 2009.

Glossary

bloom (BLOOM): To bloom is to open up. Cherry trees bloom in Washington, DC.

coat of arms (KOHT uhv ARMS): A coat of arms is a shield or other design that is a symbol for a family, state, or other group. Washington, DC's flag is based on George Washington's coat of arms.

district (DISS-trikt): A district is an area. The District of Columbia is the same piece of land as the city of Washington.

jazz (JAZ): Jazz is a type of music where musicians add notes in unexpected places. Duke Ellington, who was born in Washington, DC, played jazz.

justice (JUSS-tiss): Justice is fair behavior. A woman on the Washington, DC quarter stands for justice.

memorial (muh-MOR-ee-ul): A memorial is a place or thing that honors people or events. The Lincoln Memorial is one of the many memorials in Washington, DC.

monument (MON-yuh-munt): A monument is an object that honors a person or an event. The Washington Monument is in Washington, DC.

motto (MOT-oh): A motto is a sentence that states what people stand for or believe. Washington, DC's motto is "Justice For All."

politics (POL-uh-tiks): Politics is the activity involved in governing. Many people in Washington, DC work in politics.

popular (POP-yuh-lur): To be popular is to be enjoyed by many people. The Lincoln Memorial is a popular place to visit in Washington, DC.

seal (SEEL): A seal is a symbol a state or district uses for government business. A statue of George Washington is on Washington, DC's seal.

statue (STACH-oo): A statue is a model of a person made out of metal or rock. The Lincoln Memorial includes a statue of Abraham Lincoln.

symbols (SIM-bulz): Symbols are pictures or things that stand for something else. The seal and flag are Washington, DC's symbols.

tourism (TOOR-ih-zum): Tourism is visiting another place (such as a state or country) for fun or the jobs that help these visitors. Many people in Washington, DC work in tourism.

tours (TOORZ): Tours are sightseeing trips. Visitors to Washington, DC often take tours.

Further Information

Books

Aaseng, Nathan. *The White House*. San Diego, CA: Lucent Books, 2001.

O'Neal, Claire. *Class Trip: Washington, D.C.* Hockessin, DE: Mitchell Lane Publishers, 2010.

Smith, Marie, and Roland Smith. *N is for Our Nation's Capital: A Washington, DC Alphabet*. Chelsea, MI: Sleeping Bear Press, 2005.

Web Sites

Visit our Web site for links about Washington, DC: *childsworld.com/links*

Note to Parents, Teachers, and Librarians: We routinely verify our Web links to make sure they are safe and active sites. So encourage your readers to check them out!

Index